Katie Woo's Silly School Jokes

Based on characters created by Fran Manushkin

edited by Blake Hoena

illustrated by Tammie Lyon

PICTURE WINDOW BOOKS
a capstone imprint

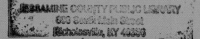

Katie Woo is published by Picture Window Books,
A Capstone Imprint
1710 Roe Crest Drive
North Mankato, Minnesota 56003
www.mycapstone.com

Cataloging-in-Publication Data is available on the Library of
Congress website.

ISBN: 978-1-5158-0974-6 (library binding)
ISBN: 978-1-5158-0978-4 (paperback)
ISBN: 978-1-5158-0990-6 (eBook PDF)

Summary: Katie Woo loves to make her teacher, Miss Winkle laugh
with this collection of school-themed jokes. You can make your
classmates giggle too with knock-knocks, riddles, and more. At the
end of the book, be sure to check out Katie's joke-telling tips and
helpful glossary.

Designer: Kayla Dohmen

Printed in the United States of America.
010045S17

Table of Contents

Wacky **TEACHER** Jokes

Miss Winkle: Katie, why did you bring your dad to school today?

Katie: You said we were having a POP quiz.

What did the teacher say to the calendar?

"Your days are numbered!"

Why did the teacher cross the road?

To give the chicken a test.

Katie: We need a new substitute teacher.

JoJo: Why do you think that?

Katie: Ours doesn't know much. She keeps asking us questions.

Why did the teacher go to the beach?

To test the water.

Where did the music teacher leave his keys?

In the piano.

Miss Winkle: Katie, what was the hardest part of today's homework?

Katie: The answers.

Side-Splitting SCHOOL Jokes

When do astronauts eat at school?

LAUNCH time.

Katie: Pedro, why are you late to school again?

Pedro: I didn't catch the school bus.

Katie: Well, run faster.

What is a pirate's favorite subject in school?

ARRRRT.

Where do giants go to school?

HIGH school.

Where does ice cream go to school?

SUNDAE school.

Why are fish the smartest animals?

They stay in schools all of their lives.

What is an owl's favorite subject in school?

Bi-OWL-ogy.

I was sick yesterday, and people keep asking me if I missed school. I told them I stayed home, slept all day, and I didn't miss it one bit.

Classroom
CRACK-UPS

Knock, knock.

Who's there?

Broken pencil.

Broken pencil who?

**Oh, what's the point
of this joke?**

What flies around in the classroom at night?

Alpha-BATS.

Why can't you do your homework with a broken pencil?

Because it's pointless!

What do elves learn in school?

The ELF-abet.

Katie: JoJo, why did you eat your homework?
JoJo: Because I don't have a dog.

Knock, knock.

Who's there?

Howl.

Howl who?

Howl we ever solve this problem?

Knock, knock.

Who's there?

Dewey!

Dewey who?

**Dewey really have
more homework?**

JoJo: Katie, why are you
drawing a picture of a house?
Katie: It's my HOME-work.

When my mom asked me what I learned in school today, I told her not enough because I have to go back tomorrow.

Knock, knock.

Who's there?

Rita.

Rita who?

Rita lot of books lately?

School Subject
KNEE-SLAPPERS

What is at the end of a rainbow?

A W, of course.

Why were the Pilgrims like ants?

They lived in colonies.

Knock, knock.

Who's there?

Spell.

Spell who?

W-H-O

What is smarter than a talking parrot?

A spelling bee.

Katie, on your birthday, if you receive $10 from Pedro and $7 from JoJo, what will you get?

A new outfit!

Why did the germ walk across the microscope?

To get to the other SLIDE.

What did the number zero (0) say to the number eight (8)?

Nice belt!

Miss Winkle: Do you know the first president of the United States?
Katie: No, we were never introduced.

Why did the Pilgrims sail to the Americas?

Because it was too far to swim.

Why is 6 afraid of 7?

Because 7 8 9 (7 ate 9).

Why did Katie bring a ladder to music class?

The teacher told her
to sing higher.

Katie: Pedro, why did you eat
your math homework?

Pedro: Because Miss Winkle said
it was a piece of cake.

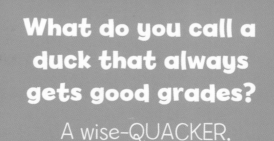

What do you call a
duck that always
gets good grades?

A wise-QUACKER.

What was the witch's favorite subject in school?

SPELL-ing.

JoJo: Did you bring a bucket
to band practice?
Katie: Why would I need a bucket?
JoJo: To carry a tune.

What was the snake's favorite class?

HISSSS-story.

Why did the nurse fail art class?

He could only draw blood.

Miss Winkle: What do you get when you multiply 72 by 46?

Katie: A headache.

Playful **PLAYGROUND** Jokes

Why did the chicken cross the playground?

To get to the other SLIDE.

Why doesn't anyone want to play soccer with Cinderella during recess?

Because she's always running away from the ball.

What do toads play at recess?

Leapfrog.

JoJo: Katie, why don't you like playing on the slides?

Katie: They're such downers.

JoJo: Have I told you the joke about the jump rope?

Katie: No, let's skip it.

HOW
TO TELL A
JOKE

Even the funniest jokes can get groans if you don't tell them right. Here are my best joke-telling tips!

Know your audience—
Everybody has a different sense of humor. That means different things make different people laugh. My friends like jokes about school and gross things. My grandparents think jokes about old stuff are a hoot. So I pick jokes that my audience is sure to laugh at.

by Katie Woo

Know your material—I memorize my jokes. I like to stand in front of a mirror and practice the joke until I know it by heart. That way I know I'll do a good job when I'm ready to tell it to someone.

Timing—Most jokes have two parts. The setup says what the joke is about, and the punch line is the funny part. Here's an example:

Setup: When do astronauts eat at school?
Punch line: LAUNCH time.

After I say the setup, I'm always excited to blurt out the punch line right away. But I stop myself. Instead, I take a deep breath and slowly count "one-banana, two-banana" in my head. That way my audience has time to think about the joke. If they don't answer by two-banana, then I shout the punch line. Ha!

Katie Woo's
stories keep the laughs going!

Katie Woo — Cartwheel Katie

Katie Woo — The Best Club

Katie Woo — Cowgirl Katie

Katie Woo — Katie and the Fancy Substitute!

THE FUN DOESN'T STOP HERE!

Discover more at www.capstonekids.com

- Videos & Contests
- Games & Puzzles
- Friends & Favorites
- Authors & Illustrators

Find cool websites and more books like this one at www.facthound.com.

Just type in the Book ID:

9781515809746

and you're ready to go!